Spending the Light

ALSO BY TOM SMITH

POETRY

 Some Traffic (Beyond Baroque Foundation, 1976)
 Singing the Middle Ages (The Countryman Press, 1982)
 Traffic (Harry Smith, 1984)
 The Broken Iris (Persephone Press, 1991)
 Waiting on Pentecost (Birch Brook Press, 1999)
 Cow'sleap: a Nightbook (Fithian Press, 1999)
 Trash: the Dahmer Sonnets (Red Moon Press, 2000)

NOVEL

 A Well-Behaved Little Boy (Woldt, 1993)

Spending the Light

(Poems 1955–2003)

Tom Smith

2004 / FITHIAN PRESS
MCKINLEYVILLE, CALIFORNIA

Published by Fithian Press
A division of Daniel and Daniel, Publishers, Inc.
Post Office Box 2790
McKinleyville, CA 95519
www.danielpublishing.com

LIBRARY OF CONGRESS CATALOGING-IN-PUBLICATION DATA
Smith, Tom, (date)
 Spending the light : poems / by Tom Smith.
   p. cm.
 ISBN 1-56474-434-5 (pbk. : alk. paper)
 I. Title.
 PS3569.M5384S65 2004
 811'.54—dc22
      2003014184

remembering my parents

The following poems have been published in periodicals as cited: "Walking in Snow: to Gertrude Stein" and "Stanzas on My Name" in *Virginia Quarterly Review* (1959); "Walking in Snow" also anthologized in *Content with the Example: A Gertrude Stein Companion*, ed. Bruce Kellner (Greenwood Press 1988); "Stanzas on My Name" reprinted in *Best Articles and Stories* (1960); "For my Grandfather, For my Father, and For Me" and "March 1960" in *Chicago Review* (1963); "Bric a Brac," "Crickets," and "Logos" in *Far Point* (1970); "Omnibus" in *The Smith* (1972); "Supermarket," "An Afternoon with Edward Sabotka," "Perspectives," and "Camels" in *Beyond Baroque* (1972, 1974, 1979, & 1980); "Valentine" in *Dark Horse* (1981); "Medusa" in *Northern New England Review* (1982); "Thamus, Great Pan is Dead" and "Bering Strait" in *Pulpsmith* (1983 & 1984); "Queen of the Middlesex County Workhouse" and "Leaving the Campus" in *Bay Windows* (April & August 1984); "Buying Condoms" in *Beloit Poetry Journal* (1984, also anthologized in 1985 *Anthology of Magazine Verse and Yearbook of American Poetry*); "Roi Pecheur" in *Fag Rag* (1987); "Glass," "Weeding," and "Young Raccoon" in *Blueline* (1988); "Letter to my Mother" in *The Carrell* (1990); "Two for Julian and Ben" in *Jeopardy* (1991); "Brother Joseph" in *The Northern Review* (1991); "Albany Street 1939" in *Poetry Motel* (1994).

Contents

Envoys

PROEM

Walking in Snow: to Gertrude Stein
(1955)

I

This evening children in the street have run
out of their mittens making lovely men
of snow. From odds and ends of coal a stare
and grin that little hands leave guardian
exclude our praise surrendering to prayer.
Hello, Ms Stein. And when you left your chair
beside the fire, walking in the snow
you made discovery of prayer for fun
that once upon a time. Hello, hello,
Ms Stein, hello: the variations fall
into the snow as you repeat them all.

II

We often see a picture of Ms Stein:
The hills have gardens on them and the lawn
is growing up behind her back and she
of course is seated and surrounded on
all sides;—but truthfully we do not see
the gardens on the hills and truthfully
we do not see the grass. The rocker waits
to carry her away; meanwhile, serene
and distant as a snowfall, she excites
our love of solitude, for she is round
and full of private fun in repetend.

III

The children in the street know how to play,
know how to pack the falling snow away
behind the snowmen's eyes. The children take
the weather in their arms exceedingly
and roll it up; and that is how to make
an image, finding fun in every flake
of snow, heroic comedy, to pack
the formless drift of every happy day

into a bright and private globe of fact.
Comedienne of days, Ms Stein can show
us how to make a snowman out of snow.

The way to build a snowman is through prayer
in repetend. Ms Stein has written for
our eyes considerable snowfalls bold
to keep their secrecy of sense: the more
the story of a life is left untold
the more we give ourselves; in time we build
our snowmen and our saints. The greatest fun
I find on looking into Stein whose sure,
exclusive grin won't let a stranger in,
the greatest invitation: she forsakes
the pleasure; therefore, I may write her books.

IV
The children have gone home. Heaven allows
the snowfall through the stars turning our eyes
adrift that follow as it folds in air,
then seems to break away from earth, from trees,
circling back upon some celibate star.
Wafers of snow to earth administer
their sacrament fading into our flesh,
burdening the sky with little honesties
from heaven. Now and then the wind will flash
out of the trees establishing a throne
of air that keeps the snowfall, coming down.

My heart is full of longing after snow;
for there is so much earth and so much sky
meeting the drift behind my eyes that turn
aside to follow the snowfall down. I go
out walking; for the storm is my concern,
is mine. The snowfall coming down is mine,
is my most secret blessing and my wound
of everyday. I wish, if I can pray,
to give back good of unsuspected kind,

a subtle ecstacy like snow. The air,
this night, becomes my guardian of prayer:

how can we know it is snowing, how can we know;
how can we know it is snowing, vastly snow
and vastly snowing, vastly knowing: can
we know: how can we know; for there is so

much sky, how can we know; how can a man
expressly hope to know: what can be known:
how can we know, how can the snow be vast,
how can the sky be vast: how can we know
it is snowing, how can we know; and how express
our knowing it is snowing if we know:
how can we know, how can we know the snow.

Words can become the thing itself. I lift
the snowfall outward from my heart, adrift,
to take up flesh enforcing solitude.
A snowflake cherishes its form, the soft,
hermetic pattern of the ghost obscured
in quietude of size. My words exclude
another's eyes. My flesh is commonplace,
or seems, like snow. My ghost remains: the gift
of prayer and puzzle of my happy days;
for words make visible the world, the rhyme,
the measure of its harmony and form.

      V
We take the weather in our arms like song
turning digressions of our days along
a white periphery up from the drift
of snow: days pass. The children do no wrong
establishing a form drawn from the shaft,
collapsible, of faded air to lift
up lovely men of snow. I see that they
are unaware of me. They are among
some wing of angels singing pointlessly,

for they are at their game and, knowing how
to play out prayer, their flesh is turned to snow.

So, reader, in the snow, do not invade
my prayer. Our blank encounters are well made
to pass without hello. Allow my way
in isolated sacrament, applied
to stars, for it must keep its secrecy.
Give me farewells. As I release a day
of little bliss into the sky, don't breathe
it down into the drift before it plays
its circuit of my heart. Days pass; the earth
turns on itself. So, reader, you will do
me well; and I will do the same for you.

Hello, Ms Stein, farewell. We will do well
together keeping to ourselves. The fall,
the swell of snow recalls your hermitage
in words, clean to invasion, simple,
white and white as snow, as snowfall, page
on page of comedy and prayer, as sage,
opaque, as days. Ms Stein, your eyes and grin
exclude a friend as you extend to all
the courtesy of fun. Farewell, Ms Stein.
Days pass; the world turns on itself like snow.
This is the most exclusive prayer I know.

I. TOWN

Letter to my Mother

When first I wintered, in your womb,
you were not rinded like an orange.
Afterwards the room that I was peeled into
was not a blazing orchard.
You had asked for brilliant oranges,
but oranges were dear,
the nation's whole economy was black, and you
were pregnant facing in the Five and Dime the girls
and customers until on Christmas Eve you quit
and joined your handsome husband out of work,
his catatonic mother,
and his father drunk.
The dark comes early from December until March,
but could not hide the darkness in the house.
You were afraid.
You couldn't keep a boarder anymore
who never paid his rent.
Then I was bodily evicted.
Darkness stayed.

When I was small I had a yellow cat.
The cat was fat and sleepy.
I'd sit and hold him on my lap
whole afternoons.
The wooden step beneath me glowed.
The fat slow sun sat in the sky.
The cat slept in my lap
and did not try to get away.
The summer I was ten I could not sleep.
Every night, while something selfish hid
beneath my bed, I tossed weeping.
Then you came from the lighted kitchen.
You can't be blamed
that, when you said there's nothing to be afraid of,
you were not convincing. Something darkness made
came nervous with you to my side. I slept no better
though you left the door ajar to let the kitchen in.

A shadow lurks behind the sun each dawn.
You carried the Great Depression in your body.
I was born. The house was mad.
You were afraid. The world was bad.
Could you prevent a madhouse from your narrow bed?
Sometimes a yellow cat suffices and we've sunny days.
Sometimes my heart and hunger know how darkness stays.

For my Grandfather, for my Father, and for Me

1. If such a jug as jigging Jim might carry
to his workingday were mine and all Jim's swearing
filled my legs with crowing, I would spare

no ear and even you would hear of cocky
Jim in his socks laughing up an old stocking
and whiskey and beer where he got his tears like flocks

of fat crows cawing, weeping to show he was friendly
as he put his lush cronies through walls never bending
his knees for the throw and roaring made his ends.

He was a gentle man whose fists, great hairy
lovers, were swains of the heart's daring
to be a muscle and the man a dear.

2. Jim was my father's father, full of plucky
Irish born. He never finished joking
in the morning. All night he sang and swore his luck.

He worked two boats on the Erie with Blacks, two dandy
mules named Shandy and Ho for the towing and
his money-making almost matched his spending

until he sank them both to make a landing
one time his roaring thirst got out of hand
and threw the mules in after, Ho and Shandy.

Getting and spending Jim could work the back
off any man until the time of breaking
loose with a foot too wide and a throat as mucky.

3. Jim was a roofer standing and I was four
in my father's hands watching Jim straddle squaring
his great short legs in the wind, singing and story-

making. I let go my father's hand.
I was four. Jim was a roofer standing.
We were three of us and the sky was windy.

Albany Street 1939

Halsey Elementary School
burdened a corner of Albany and Steuben.
Its coketown brick and granite sills
brooded over concrete and the hard
dirt of the playground. Stone stairs,
inside brick caverns, climbed to doors
too heavy for a tardy kindergartner.
The whole pile felt as bolted to the earth
as our desks and chairs
were bolted to the hardwood floors
inside. Its mass and ogre
darkness made a statement: all
schools are reform schools.
I'll bet it's standing still.

We were all six or seven in first grade.
I lived in a crooked flat on Craig Street,
two blocks north, two blocks
closer to the top of the long hill leaning
downtown toward the movies and the river.
Patty lived next door: a rogue
girl like the bandit woman's daughter in *The Snow
Queen*. Across the street
were Emil whose mother was a whore,
lewd Newel who bullied his parents.
The next street down was Hulett
where Draper's and Brownell's father
ministered his flock of black methodists and Saul
slept over his father's kosher meats.

Between Craig and Steuben was Hamlin.
Marty lived on Hamlin.
I was in love with Marty
and a girl named Barbara Sawyer
whose many brothers and sisters were grown up
and in high school or graduated

to GE or American Locomotive. In my family,
one aunt had been through high school.
She worked in a laundry. On the corner
of Hamlin was a bicycle shop
with unattainable, delaying displays
of shining Schwinns and games
(Monopoly, Parcheesi) and books
about Winnie the Pooh
and Peter Rabbit.

On the corner of Craig was a Jewish bakery:
rye bread, raisin cookie, jelly doughnut.
Along the blocks: three bars, an A&P,
a German pork store, bowling alley,
candy store and newsroom selling numbers,
paint store, hardware, apartments, and a few
two-families, their clapboard
braving stone.

I lived with my parents of course
and the small brother hanging from my arm.
Our backyard was a square of hard black dirt
in which nothing would grow.
The other yards on Craig were deeper and dustier
ending in leaning garages. Marty's backyard,
on grassy tree-lined Hamlin, flooded in spring
and in autumn filled with bees and the smell
of dropped pears. Stray fruit
trees survived,
more or less wild,
in the lots and narrow alleys
behind garages backing on garages.
I think we got drunk on cherries,
their red rinds rich as nightmares.
The apple tree where Marty and I sailed
our afternoons has somehow rooted
my grownup dreamworld, many-armed
as goddesses, scarred and starry as the cosmos.

We could almost walk along its boughs.

Fall, winter, spring,
four times daily,
mobs of rowdies,
tomboys and sissies,
five to twelve,
tramped the cracked blocks breaking
mothers' or devils' backs.
We kicked through leaf heaps looking
for a ruby or golden fallen star.

We trekked the Alp and Himalaya banks
like goats. I lived in fear of snowballs.
Once I had mittens for two days.
I was warm in the mackinaw my mother
made of a wool blanket, a plaid
of yellow, green, and rusted orange.
We broke out roller skates and ropes and marbles.
The girls said girls are best:
Christ's mother was a girl. The boys
looked embarrassed thinking God
was a boy. In my fancy
we are bright as gumdrops or M&M's.
We bob and jostle like balloons.
We'd easily float off.
We may have been a little sticky,
but we didn't melt in anybody's hands.
In fact, we were rather
drab, scrappy and tacky, trashy
brats, our people,
more or less poor, hanging
at the far edge of the Great Depression.
In three years we would fall into the war.

One noon I climbed the iron ladder to the top,
terra incognita, infirma,
of sixth graders, swung

over the rail and hung
by my ankles above the playground crowd
while they looked up at me
and I looked down my nose at racing clouds.
I seem to hear a timebomb ticking: we were going
to be a terrible generation. But in spring '39,
Marty and I, truant,
tore half his cellar door off its hinges
and rafted the Mississippi of his yard—
pear blossoms floating
and reflected on icy water
and my brother bawling on the shore.
I think we reached the gulf
and mad Sargasso.

Brother Joseph

I hung at the kitchen window
of my parents' flat and, watching
my brother with his buddies
playing ball, prayed god
to strike him down.
Making myself the puppet
master of the Punch
and Judy world I tried
to lift the dusty Ford that passed between us
and the ball he chased into the street
to a climactic vector: *momentum mortis*.
Nothing went right.
I lost my self-respect and faith
to the eventless dusty afternoon. A year
later I took his name at confirmation,
discontinued catechism,
left the church.

At thirteen and eleven, for a little
while, both friendless in a new
neighborhood, we shared
a sled some winter evenings between pines. A nice
indifference of trees allowed us through. One Saturday
at the movies our hands
touched slipping greasy in one bag
of popcorn. Some dirty
old man had groped
his way into my pants in the lubricious
dark, but Joey didn't know.

When I learned from my unhappy mother
he was blowing his enviable scholarship coming home
before completing his first semester, I wrote him:
"Playing basketball is your poetry.
Stay with the call of your flesh
and spirit. The world does not

often make room for love's work."
I never mailed the letter.

Joey died of a massive heart
attack at thirty-seven
leaving his widow well-provided and a pretty
daughter, five years old.
I had been sober
six months. Mother
called to tell me, asked me to attend
the funeral, timid, apologetic,
afraid I might not come.

You ought to know
he did go back to college. Look:
he stands six/four in the brief
uniform they wear. His vast feet,
Huckleberry rafts, and thighs,
a renaissance of skill and perspiration,
push off a hard floor. See
him soar and turn on air. His long,
dumb arms reach up.
He's a cathedral
and just right
his eagle wrist
breaks the gold egg
into the basket.

The Circumcision

Grade four was a battle
of the sexes: he—unreachable
sleeping beauty waiting
for a kiss to wake him woman;
Mrs. Buchanon, crown of thorns, determined
he should be a boy. Though daily
she'd point him out among his peers
wagging her stout
finger behind his wiggle: *is that*
a walk? and nod
heavily as the class
shrilled over him fallen
on the playground: *Maryjane!*
still he would show up Hallowe'en
in lipstick and his mother's dress.
Mrs. Buchanon and the principal at last
called his mother to the office:
something will have to be done
about Tommy. The school
physician shrugged and suggested
circumcision. Tommy dreamed
for seven nights of the kiss
of the princely knife. Another seven
nights he dreamed of milkweed
pods exploding in shadow. The platinum
silk took flight.

I can remember very little
concerning the event: the bath
my mother gave me standing
me naked on a chair beside the zinc
blue kitchen sink. The blushing
Lifeboy lathering between my legs:
this little piggy went to market.
Also the redhead nurse whose laughter
teased me out of weeping as I came

from the anesthetic dark where time
and space caved in on dreams
and nothing was.

Tommy could remember only Tommy's eyes
that watched the milkweed mouth float
down to meet his gradual
dissolving
husk.

Roi Pecheur

The last math problem
every evening seemed
forever while I counted
fingers thinking
of Marty throbbing
at the dead end
of the mine-shaft
alley between garages
behind Boone's
Apartments—Marty
waiting for me.

What did mouth measure?
What did eye-teeth see?
Sunday morning's gold
and jeweled aspergill
made flesh. The fish
at the end of the line.

March 1960

Come, strong and straight young man from Coca Cola,
wind up my springs and pump my little Victrola.
I really love the way you park your truck.
You stride into the shop and turning your back
slip the cases from your great big shoulder
onto the floor, firm handler, handsome. "Soldier!"

The gal behind the counter watches. "Fella!"
she shouts. "When I was young and slenderella,
you'd take me in one hand and drink me up
like a bottle of Coke." Oh, the wide brown grip!
She shouts and shouts. She used to be a stripper
until she got too fat to fit a zipper.

Thus over coffee you have found me sitting.
For my singing we could find no larger setting.
The fatgirl shouting backward to her youth
for the man from Coca Cola who in truth
is young and fills the shop within our hearing
with his breathing where the life comes with him rearing.

    Tomorrow is my birthday. Spring
    is two days later. Everything
        is ready. I would rather
    stay, all winter for my brow
    a cover have of silent snow,
        than have to meet that weather.

    Spring is sweet, her coming fair
    with little birds that fill the air.
        She does not last forever.
    Her season is too much with time,
    too hurried in the flesh. She came
        before, before; however,

I will be twenty-seven. Then,
how shall I wear my body when
    I see her blossoms glisten?
Sweet Spring! Sweet Spring's a little slut
and I'll be twenty-seven, but
    (listen, lover, listen)

along the street that's wet from rain
the stallion canters by again,
    the cop is in his saddle.
The stallion's back is very broad
and shines because it is so hard,
    magnificent to straddle.

Antimuse

My way was occupied
by an enormous dog
approaching with his hag,
and I am terrified
of ancient women. So
I stopped at once beside
a graveyard gate and tried
to think where I might go.

Then slyly, petrified
that she might say good day,
I turned out of my way.
The graveyard gate complied.

I heard how every tree
observed a breeze and sighed.
This whispered colloquy
ignored my presence quite
as if I'd stayed outside.

The hag was out of sight
I saw, but I delayed.
The graveyard was so fair
I felt I was not there.
So absently I strolled.

A breeze from mound to mound
disturbed the leaves but tried
in vain to move the sun
which slumbered satisfied
to have all afternoon.

Then down the road I heard
some dreadful brake applied.
Whether the hag was killed
or not, grass may decide.

Medusa

I'd want to have missed her face
but cutting the crosstown pace
from Forty-Second Street
I missed instead my feet
and failed to reach Times Square
before I saw her.
Her face like stone addressed
my face with dust.

Her face was all at least
the broad and human beast,
hardest where it is torn:
pity and fear and scorn.

Then I was turned to stone
and found the crowd. Lonely
Times Square blew several horns.

Thamus, Great Pan is Dead

Caught by one hand mangled
in the stirrup, cramping speed
beneath us crashing, strangled
hemorrhoids must bleed,
thighs shiver, apprehensive,
unwilling, quick, defensive,
through token, inexpensive
graves we transit need.

Nightly I voyage, homing,
14th Street to Park Slope,
while rapidest entombing
exasperates like hope
whose noises slash reflection:
lecture, text, infection,
fever—half-erection
as brains take heat and grope.

When Swinburne's weary zephyrs
got wind of Walter Watts,
I yawned for scattered heifers,
green grapes and marble pots.
I searched the tweed professor:
Ah, father! Oh, confessor!
Oh, savior! Ah, oppressor!
Achilles' choice? or lots?

Our screams beneath the river
announce the death of Pan,
or Zeus and dam deliver
a stone for the old man.
Well, what's another slaughter?
Uranus, in hot water,
brought up a hag-born daughter
the night that time began.

Bright tigers make forever
more tigers. Do we dare?
(With sinews hot and clever
I crouched above Times Square.
The gods, like oceans churning
across the bay, discerning
my torch of license burning,
brought mortal tides to bear.)

"Live dull or die, Achilles,"
the firmament declares.
Swinburne, I lift, and lilies,
from vomit on the stairs
to prospects dark and stricken.
The new gods, Puerto Rican,
are gangsters too, and thicken
around our blond affairs.

My gelded tabby, keeping
a thunder where he nods,
awaits me. He is sleeping
while, lewd, the squadcar prods.
Like bullets, ambulances
excite, and blood enhances
the splayed and sutured glances
of cruising Goldenrod.

Queen of the Middlesex County Workhouse

We played gin all day,
Tanya and Jo and I
and Coco, cellmates
segregated in cellblock B
for our protection.

Tanya and Jo and Coco
had been busted in drag
at a social club picnic
more than a year ago.
There had been a murder
at the picnic and they all
had records; so—
the judge
had slapped the long sentence on them.

After dinner, Coco
withdrew to her *boudoir*
to prepare for her evening appearance.
I'd hang at the door to watch
and listen. "Miss Cat,
a queen has got to have money.
I can sew my own drag but
you know what wigs cost, Honey,
or a merry widow?
You can ask five dollars
but get the money first.
You tell them you got the rag on
but you'll munch them for five.
Of course there's those
will want to fuck you anyway.
The johns are pigs."

She saves burnt matches to line her eyes.
She knots the open shirt over her navel,
ruffles baggy pants with rubber bands,

pinches brown cheeks and bites her lips to color,
combs out her afro, waits—
When all the men from A have got their seats
in front of the TV, she makes her entrance
on naked, incredible feet.

It was like moonrise over the city dump.
Several would have saved a seat beside their own
and hiss for her: *come to me, Baby.*
She'd circulate, ignoring guards, trustees,
and, at lights out, mince back
to her *single*, pockets
full of candy, cigarettes
she'd share with Tanya.
They were sisters.
Jo, nineteen, enjoyed
the favors of a trustee.

They had nothing, you see,
no coin, no visitor,
clean out of relatives
or friends. No one
answered the letters they sent out,
no one considered their appeals.
They were alone
making their way
and the rest
was the dump, the rest
was the city dump.

Omnibus

We sweated on the world's hot curb.

Behind us and plate glass the air
conditioned mannequins foretold the cuts
and colors of the Fall, their slick
stiff faces, polished forests
no man hunts.

The bus, a breadloaf, baked in traffic.
The women bore the burdens of their shopping,
hipped and breasted, damp
on their ancient feet. The rusty priest,
a face like thawing beef,
guarded his fat luggage. My polaroids
reflected my ten toes and paved heat
spreading from bruised sandals.
We waited. Slices of life!

The bus arrived like after-dinner music
at an old men's home. The doors dragged open,
blunt reluctant gas. The plump priest plowed
that wet crowd of women, pushing through
them, crashing prowed. They looked—
mornings after on the mountain
sides of some old world—askance.
My shaved heels met the pavement.

He clutches between his shirt and coat a pint
and drinks from his armpit like a sparrow preening,
coming through the rye. Think of it straight
and warm, the base of the spine, this heat!
He thinks he is secret. We all see him,
even me behind my wine-dark glasses, crouch
and push the dry bottle toward the driver's seat.

Some matron like a crow behind me coughs.
"Do you think it will rain?"

Camels

On an outing (Spring '63)
at The Catskill Game Farm
with my lover and his kids
I first saw camels real.

The girl and her baby brother
pressed the fence
trying to tempt
the ruminating mother and her calf
with limp green, stale saltine.
Their brown bag, nearly deep
as they were, seemed
to swallow their brown arms.
I stood behind them.
Their father, behind me,
pressed my buttock
adulterously.
No one was looking he assumed.

I pointed out the patriarchal male.
That self-esteem enthroned on straw
at a distance in shed and shade
measured us all bored
above the nose that slowly turned
the measured cud and eternal
return of dusty afternoon and human
offering and foolish neighbor:
llama or yak.

His cow and son
reposed in the proud
vacancy of his unresponsive eye.
We stood before him and my lover
breathed kisses down my back
between my flesh and sweatshirt.
Where is he now?

God, where are they?
She must be twenty-one, her brother
sweet nineteen. Alas, brown bag.
Camels are very strange animals.

I've been thinking about camels for three days.

Don't know what started me, what chance
remark or gesture, remembering for instance
the belching, blathering chorus in *Lawrence*
that first brought my attention to the beast;
or the sepia print
torn from some book
that Marianne Moore
sent to my college buddy in response
to his ventured admiration;
the plastic miniature belonging to my sons
I dug up making a garden of their sandpile.

Then, today,
a postcard comes from friend of the family
Billy: "Benin City, May 11: See you
very soon. I'm dying.
L—, B. May 14: Alive
again." which means
perhaps we won't see him as soon.

NIGERIA. EMIR'S MUSICIANS AT DURBAR.
I look and they of course are perched
with their buff drums high
on muzzled camels.
Where am I?

II. SUPERMARKET (1968)

1. The Sandbox Tree

My name is Greentree.
Hard and dry.
The gods give this and that.

The head on my shoulders hangs inches from the white porcelain of the coffee cup. The woman and the children are sleeping. The dew. My body and the house. I am the house. My hair is a small garden attached to the house. This morning is a ram caught in my hair. My lips thought hell a fable—flowers are like that—but the morning has changed their mind. My nostrils are an attic stairs. The windows overlook a rock garden and wait for the withering sun. In my sandstone ears the dragons guard ancient manuscripts that crumble at a touch. A dead fish blooms in my mouth. My throat is a hole in the ground. Behind my eyes, fat aged carps, my brain is the surface of the moon. A serpent—
    That day the tree fell. Friday morning—
    September. Bright and dark. White metal blinds splinter. Yet, yet a moment we attend the stillborn dawn. The sun is sick. An owl. The village is six miles to the west. A town is twelve miles to the east. The directions are approximate with no symbolic value. Now, while I hang on the porcelain brink, trucks sprawl eastward, westward, and deliver—

Listen—a child. We laid the wood in order.
The mountain waited. "Let him go!"
A bird's flutter.
I heard a child singing.
A clod. A bird. A wolf. A bee. A rainbow.
The child sang, "There's the border."
The guards sang, "Halt—" Their rifles rang out. No.
The sun continued I remember.
Let it be now.
A flower. Forever.
I heard a child singing.

Two urns. The gods roar scalded from the tub.
The toilet clanks and closes. Beelzebub

in armor shudders in the floor. Me—stripped
to scale. The arrow shivers, points. A crypt,
a font, a throne, the dew, a bower. Toes
expand and shrivel, eyes and fingers close,
pores open. Here I am. Cosmetic oils
of rose and olive glitter, soda boils,
erupts. An awful rainbow. I appoint
these lights to wash the body and anoint.
The body soaks while gilded clouds decay.

    The girl who saw the morning sun
    has felt the silent current run
    beneath her. On the bank a thunder
    rings the infant's crown. That's done.
    She stripped the orchard bare—gone under.
    These ripples riddle time and pun.

Ransack the surf. Deliver yesterday.
To reach this goal I needed neither ships
nor act of will. I stutter at the lips
of springs and horns. Dull catalogs. The rounds
of soap and sun. The ancient foe has drowned
and leaps into the fisher's thankless hands.
What flowers mean—the stunned flesh understands.

From the east the trucks pound westward toward the village.
From the west the trucks burst eastward toward the town.
They are instant with loud voices in the house.
They resolve me of all ambiguities. The dew.

      The arrow. The target.
    Dimly certain shapes suggest a motion. Flight.
    Certain motions tend to shape and fascinate
    my head and dullest occupation.
    Arrow, flight, and target make the day.

    I fill the instant cup. Hot water
    mingles blessings, ills, and buds,

creating, uncreating,
darkness. There she stands. She runs
into the net and she is given.
My head clears. What is left? The porcelain.
The pool reflects
my face, a whiskered bludgeon like a catfish,
hanging and mean as a meaning in the catalog
of common things. Where is the lamb?
The goat I promised. Where is the white goat?

A cup of coffee.
What can I do?
Stay hard to get and dry.

I weigh five pounds less than I weighed last week.
I weigh ten pounds more than I weighed last year.
I love the ideal constancy of documents—
my driver's license.

The gods dream I am real.
They pluck at my garment
and whisper from the east
and from the west the trucks
deliver—

He comes. He comes. He comes. The neighbors weep gnats, I
whisper to the sandstorm, but the doctors can find no cause of
death in him. I am my own contestant. Pikes themselves betray.
The dew covers the mountains, flayed September, and the wolf.
That day the tree fell. Friday morning—

War and the blood of men surrounds the mountains. We dwell
with the mountains and the mountains cover us. The dust and
silence of crones and prophets join my body to the house where
faces throb like insect pulses. Faces float and bob in haunted
surfaces.

Bloodless fingers cross their lips. Blood-dark fingers crawl
upon their throats. They drown. The house is a sandbox tree of
mouths. And we are sandflea motes. We hover and buzz on incon-

venient wings that hold us slanting to the windows, conspiratorial, askance. The highway brings the thunder. The highway takes the thunder away. It seems we have made the journey. We have arrived safely. My hand lets the curtain fall. The gods at length give the unhappy race the honors of a grave and we are ignorant with mountains.

Well then—let it be.

The aspirin dissolves on my tongue. I sweat before the mirrored tabernacle. My stung hand holds the throbbing hive aloft. I stretch my tribute gills and cheeks beneath revolting bees. The ram is shorn and free. In the kitchen the woman shapes her morning service, damning the toaster and the loaf. Atonements, resurrections. The children are awake and crying. Now—

2. The Aspergill

Teaching is the oldest profession. It was Eve's.
And I am early. The classroom floor seesaws.
I balance desks and windows. The skeleton
and I confer. He floats on a stainless gibbet,
ochre-boned, one-armed, articulated
stainlessly with nuts and bolts. I wait,
Professor Greentree with Professor Fool,
my colleague and conspirator, and feel
the fruit swell, ripe and wet, behind my eyes.

My forehead labors. My empty stomach yawns
and student names and faces brown my tongue,
a cud of rosters, rooms. There have been rooms.
The crumble. The drift. The plaster atmosphere.
That closet of stifled birds. The skylit loft.
The stairwell—an echoing screw. My caterpillar
days and nights revolved. I plowed the moon
and sapped the root of strangers. Then I was dry!
The caves. The cafeterias. The caskets.

Here I am early. The walls are cinderblock.
The greenboard and the yellow chalk are April
in the grass. The stupid hornets beat the ceiling
with chalkdust knees. The room is a walled garden.
Outside—September smokes in boughs and barrows.
We need a golden anchor and some earth.

And even now the students rise from beds
or breakfasts. We are ready. Professor Fool
titters. "Chaste Beauty, stretch out loving hands."
Snakes and dandruff spoil my brown shoulders.
The apple glitters on my fingertips.
Our stomachs, growling, lisp at Adam. "Pluck it!"

> The fisher is wading in ashes.
> If I spit in his path, will the flashing

of lightning bring thundering
rain? If I blunder,
will the fisher still wade in the ashes?

In the rhyme of Jack and Jill, a pastoral allegory, we find that surprising synthesis of opposites which, together with economy, characterizes the highest literary art. Here is a gathering of the purest archetypes beneath a shading of colloquial innuendo: chiaroscuro, discordia concors. Jack and Jill—their names are clearly emblematic of the universal male and female: daughter of Adam, son of Eve. For hill read Paradise and Zion. See Psalms and Dante. Note the ambiguity of crown. The action is simply to ascend and fall. The wheel.—*Still the sun climbs. Bring me a pail of water.*— Etiology is suppressed. We are faced with blank chronology, coordination. The fall is inevitable and Jill's dependence absolute. Female with male, subject with king, nature with man, passion with reason, man with God—all tumble down: allegory, trope, and anagoge. Fused to this rather frigid vision, we are happy to discover, is the motive of the quest, poignant by contrast. Do they climb toward a well, deceptive pit, or spring of spiritual regeneration? These silences say more than words. See Lycidas. And pail is just too nervous to discuss. Imagine it.

> Swinging between the couple.
> Catching the light.
> Reflections...

Dandelions choke the greenboard.
Meanwhile
I squeeze among limbs and sprawling
faces, stumbling over bursting denim
bags and vinyl scrub,
returning papers. I bark at random.
"Where should we go?" Sharks dive.
The surface gathers. I step on several toes.
Fringed faces follow the sun. "Where are we?"
My numb elbows collide with certain skulls.
"Where have we been?"
The axe edge of corrasable bond descends.

The woolen sleeve darkens with hair oil.
"How can we turn? We are spinning."
Blossoms.
Blossoms.

Wildflowers burn. Chalkdust excites the clock.
I dip the aspergill. The pelvis echoes.
Professor Fool looks back. The pigeons smack
the windows. Then the students rise and walk.

3. The Sack

Meridian stands baffled at the fall
and my front door. A bird call,
neither sung nor swallowed, catches all
my centuries, the swift stall
lifted to the knotted finial.

Still time gets into everything.
The breath, blood, sap, rot, spring,
and song inherit. And seeds with wings.
And flesh and flowers pending.
Still the minute fixes as bees sting.

"Stand still and let me touch
your scalp," whispers the minute. In my crotch
the oriole hangs its nest. Women filch
the high sun stitch by stitch.
Eternity is too brief and asks too much.

Noon is the minute, sun's apostrophe
and stiffest aspect, the key
my hand addresses to the lock: Hi, Greentree!
Face to face and fact and fee,
my shade and day meet me.

We are not monotheists. We have felt
all absolutes. The flocks dispute our arms
and backs and chatter, feathered mums and masks
of sea foam in the crashing wheel of sense.

The stomach, stone, and scythe. The mounted sibling.
Severed head and sack. The prodigal.
The holy family. All the gods inhabit
the minute and the children of the minutes.

Still the minute burns and burns returning.
Beyond the battlefield and town, foes find

the ground is common. Son and father mourn.
"Where is the lamb?" The father, "Here I am."

The bachelor vows a white goat and a feast.
Matchless births are lighted and the thief
is crucified. The rhetor flees his hair,
his fingers, and his knees. "Take it and read."

The fish pay tribute to the dwelling host.
The woman sheds the serpent. Night attacks
the formal garden. "Ah, Mephistophilis!"
The minutes turn like words, burn and return.

      O sun,
swing clod, bird, wolf, bee, rainbow, swap
mass, sap, and spectrum—spin your sack.

Wash, bind, and clot this spilling bag
of time and be, vast tourniquet,
our knot and bob. Impress the spectrum
in your fist, seeds in the squinting clod,
and wring us, dazzled, homeward. Grab

us home—to lunch. Transcendence spun
the universe and hung the feedbag
on your nose. Be bird of prey and wolf
the world and raven, blazing maw.
Dark sponge, draw and assume the spectrum,

stew and alphabet, the gamut.
Stand, mystic of matter and motion, swap
inside the gate and mete, bold foot,
our reeling buskins and this sock,
our sagging history. Our bees

have underscored you, bumblebees,
our bards of hearths and hierarchies,
creation, fall and wall, and sack

of cities. Be our body. Sound
and chart our voyages, old eye.

First fob, outlast. Witness to clod
and clock, spin—spin us, tick and wheel.
          Take stock.

Childhood returns an empty sunshine. Toes,
solemn and stiff against a stoop edge, hinge.
The child hangs like a pocketknife folding
into itself a memory of light.

Home is a flat. The child studies his knees,
carves secret promises in sunburn scabs
with nails, and dreams of actresses and angels.
He straddles silent rails and spits in rivers.

The neighbor is a drab. The child has nuns
enhance the world with darkness and the host
adorn his need. He crosses his eyes at mass
to make the candles dance before his greed.

The backyard fence has rot. Often he digs
into the planks beneath the earth, seeking
the awful odor. Deeply he inhales
and finds a nausea which, perhaps, is me.

The child is me and I am not the child.
He reaches out. They all want to be free.
I gather in, like oaks, inhabited,
rooted in ancient sprawls of herbs and weeds.

This brass knob flashing bags the day.
Time was—I burned to flay
the planets. O hyperbole!
O suicide! The sun hauls me and our stray
bag of being through dumb space. O stay—

The respiration of each minute facets time
and springs our rhetoric. The rhyme
and ram are shorn. O crime!
O symbol! The sublime
submits to treatise. *The gods dream.*

Stay hard to get and dry. Sharks dive.
Still the sun climbs. O stricken hive!
The child and father sieve
for blossoms. I have
a pail of water. Bring me staves.

We need a virtuoso for these keys,
the play of our precise and myriad identity.
My hand will turn the day.
The door swings open. *We
are real.* Hi, Greentree!

4. The Zodiac

The children wrestle seatbelts. The woman wears
the palpitating engine like her rollers—
hood, hub, and rattle. She battles gas and gears,
taking the wheel to bury the spurned archer.

A black bull shoots the sunwhite highway.
Cumulo-nimbus.
Small insects pock the windshield.
Oaks, elms, and willows gaze,
turn giddy, rave, and die upon the hood.
The horned god brings the family to market.
The woman swells
against pressing trucks and slowpokes, pops
the uncreating word and gives her finger.
Her face is busy Lazarus behind stained glasses
where momentary fires
—fragments of crop, horse, barn,
and porch with rocker—flash and drop.
Her sunhat flaps and ultimate mountains hover.
Mountains hover, godless as the hanging
afternoon.

At the temple, Great Atlantic and Pacific Tea Company, doors open. Doors stroke the almost silent air that sways to the arrivals and departures of respectable pilgrims. The woman swings her purse, I press my palm against my breast and checkbook: tacit passports to the garden. Soaps cachinate and cheer *et luxe* delight. And roasting hens rotate. The cathedral smokes and smells. Registers ring and whirr. They reel and drawers explode against the stomachs of calculating girls. Squealing baskets rollerskate the aisles with toddlers pickaback. Blood-tight cellophane smothers steaks and chops. *What pharaohs dream beneath the pyramided cans of corned beef hash?* The secret life that dwells behind the labels. I drift among reaching hands, excellent hands and insect mystery of fingers and, driven by the tumult in my heart, seek refuge between the jolly giant's pasteboard thighs. Chinese cabbage gleams, the first high tide of the creation. The celery salutes me. Me—hagiographer of grape and eggplant, hanging belly, flapping cheek, triumphant fig and dragon too of trick and treat. The pears are sitting pretty. O oranges! I hear one singing voice of many children. The worm of comedy gnaws outward from the center of the cornucopiae of joy—a hundred thousand packed brown bags.

    The maidens shake dew from their aprons.
    The sky tumbles into their laps,
    and trees drop their blessings.
    The sun haunts the press.
    I sing of impossible apples.

Pisces. On ice, a gold and green ellipsoid,
my poetic form, the fish stares out at dead
eternity. The flat round eye is payment
and policy: the longer view that missed
the net. What will become now of his wife
and spawn? Lo—still the mouth is dumb, simple,
hungry nature. A man's most ancient instinct
is sucking. Habit attaches habitat.
The ocean tosses, dreaming, on wet sheets.

My brain, a rolling prism in slow orbit,
tosses, born of woman. I have survived
mumps, measles, chickenpox, the public schools,
won scholarships, degrees, a police record,
earn a living, easy compromise,
small sins, a woman, two small boys, a cat,
a house, an expensive lawn—inland. Inland—
Civilized man no longer holds on
to the sea. Somewhere the copepods are coping.

A fish louse scales a fish like Everest.
Poor fish. I have arrived: a child who turned
fantastic lies on bitten fingertips,
waiting for Pentecost, a burning pupil,

shoplifter, sleepless hustler, couch-patient,
inmate, graduate, and mate. Poor louse.

Failure, defeat, loss, exile, death, despair,
the toys we toss to rattling infants, I
am bawling Pisces on ice, discovering
at heart the funny man, and good for nothing
but to ask for help. Outstare and pout.
The children are amused. Where is the woman?

5. The Host

The woman and the guests attack a dip of shrimps and cheese. I balance ice cubes on my nose. "Herr Greentree—mein host." We have been to the movies and seen that motion is a matter of fixed shots. We hang behaviors on the air like talk. Chips off the old potato. "Why, what evil hath he done?" September—

Friday evening. Wit's end. With bourbon on the rocks I crown the day. A record drops. The room turns through smoke, crooning to the diamond. Small lamps illumine floor and ceiling. We are dim between. Our postures loom behind our drinks and cigarettes. Fingers flicker against the grandeur of dark mouths. Rings burn. Knees glitter beneath wool and shadow. My feet, my black socks on the carpet, make a firm and perfect end toward which all bodies move: "From walking up and down." *The Scarabaeid.* My drink floats on my palm, slow whorl of darkness spiked with tiny lights and clinking lightnings. But the glass—the walls, the lawn, the highway, and the mountains.

"Fall on us."

Herr Greentree—old herring. And the voices of the mob prevailed. The voices of the priests. We have prevailed. Grand mouths gape. Mouths weep. Cheeks quake. My feet. My feet. I feel I am in trouble with the mountains. And my feet. "Whence comest thou?"

Headlights, gliding between treetrunks, swing to the road.
Goodnight. The guests depart. I wave a winking fifth.
Behind me: open window, running water, clatter in the sink.
I sit beside the bottle on the lawn and watch the stars.

Drink up.
All heaven and my head—old haunted house.
Me—auctioneer, hawking the garden's breath.
What am I up to?
Where is Aries? Where are Gemini and Virgo,
Taurus, Capricorn? The woman is Aquarius.
Where is the enemy?
The night is cold. I do not love the moon.

Drink up.
Do I not love the moon? My daughter,
we will keep these lights awake all night.
These ancient lights. The golden fleece.
Incomprehensible antiquity gives me a twinkling.
My eyes, quick sailors, subtler
than minds or moons, invaded
by stars and older
than all time and mind, know time: instantly
bursting, instantly forming tide. All heaven.
Why then do I lie here breathing
lamentations for the drowned?
Stars swing the silent surface.
I aim the moonlit bottom of the bottle
and drink up.

Body and mind. The gods, who fill the cup,
have made us for themselves. The gods drink up.
The earth leaps up beneath my feet. I am
the garden. My body and the earth. Old ram.
The children learn to walk. Thought rests behind
the fist that lands the prophet. I can find
no enemy among these constellations.
I wage no argument with earth if nations
rise or fall. I gladly call my neighbor
civil. He sends his sons to war and labor.
"I share the banquet and consent to live."

I share the banquet and consent to live.
The private citizen. The woman and
the children, who are living by my hand,
must live with me. We have a little time.
I am the enemy. They are my crime.
Old father, do you sleep? Declare my debt.
I give the enemy his gate and get
his goat. The mountains do not give a damn.
Myself am home. And home is where I am.

Lock up the house. The bow is drawn toward heaven.
"Lay not thine hand upon the lad."
Forget. Forgiven.
Our houses stand all night.
The bowl, the lard, the leaven, and the board.
Dawn waits upon the shriving
of the beggar lord. Regard the sleeping head.
Nothing is whole. Nothing is riven.
Seek your bed.
Bright eels are weaving
the old song. Our houses stand.

Woman, woman, stretch out loving arms to welcome and embrace me. Words—that are not stone or wood or straw—are sound. The branch is cut. The bough is burned.

Words are wind. The wind supports a burden. Our words are worn and adapted to possession. Woman, woman, stretch out loving arms. We share the song. Sing. Listen. Spin and dream. We roll the cosmos and the house in our warm mouths. The branch is cut. *Terminat hora diem.* Day will begin the dream. The trees accept the wind. The shadows. Woman, woman—

The children sleep in wooden cribs. They sleep with animals. You will find them crying in the morning. The bough is burned. *Terminat hora diem.* There is always some silent fire keeping our bodies. There is always dew. Woman, woman, let me rest in you. *Terminat hora diem. Terminat—*

III. COUNTRY

Buying Condoms

Another April blew into town,
another month we discovered
it was not too late to be careful
and, the way the sap was running,
it was none too soon.

Between marriages and nearly thirty, I was shier
than the maples budding along the river
and sliming the pavement all the way up Union Street
in the spring rain. I passed the pharmacy twice: a nice
old-fashioned store looming under elms, dim and unfrequented,
three thirty in the afternoon, huge jug of colored water
in each window.

I worried what to ask for:
Trojan, Ramsey, Sheik were the only names
I knew, remembered from street corner
meetings in my teens, the alley cats,
old information of dubious authority.
I could not see myself a hector or fancy
desert rapist in a sweating tent.
I was not a scapegoat yet.
Young Boswell called it armor.
Sheath or sleeve I'd heard.
Why did prophylactic sound so nasty?
I wouldn't ask for rubbers on a rainy day.
I walked in to a giggle of small bells.

If a woman stood behind the counter, I'd buy aspirin;
though, perhaps, it would be easier, more honest really,
than having to deal with some slick guy
who'd ooze his oiled head in on the dirty joke,
our love life.
Nature really is hard knocks on romance.

I asked for condoms. The old gentleman
nodded, sober and professional.
Opening a small drawer beneath the marble counter,
he set out several brands and proceeded to explain,
words bland and simple,
the special qualities of each, a neutral
text: good health and mutual pleasure and common sense.
Finally his eyes smiled into mine: "One size fits all."
I thought he probably had sons and grandsons.
I felt good to be a man.

The sun dropped through small clouds.
I stood on the April sidewalk, stroking
the small brown bag, feeling
my lungs bloom forsythia, knowing
I was in love, grinning
about the funny girl
who was changing
my life.

Valentine

That sapling day
when slender Hansel
found the sugarhouse
the witch of course
stood waiting.

"Welcome home," she crooned.
Unhesitating he flowed
across the apple-studded
ground into her lap
while bees that hovered
around him sucked the cider
garden contemplating
their bursting knees.

The year revolved
creating a seasonable feast.
Hansel sat crowned
with parsley. Sweetheart,
here's the oven door.

Bering Strait

(These intimations are occasioned by Lennart Nilsson's
photographs in A Child is Born, *Dell 1969.*
Stanza 7 paraphrases The Encyclopedia Americana.*)*

1. The serpent saps polarities
   that ordinarily obtrude obscuring
   eternal verities.
   The serpent and the tree extend their code
   through generations, wreathing and unweaving,
   to the caducous bud, our caduceus.
   Adam wears Eve like the kelp lacing
   Aphrodite's perpetual ankles and knees.
   Our seed, a froghopper's froth beading
   milkweed, is wonderful at 26 days.
   The serpent and the tree implode.

2. The yolk and amnion rotate
   distributing inner space.
   The dawning placenta flocculates.
   The moon is great with a dolphin.
   Light freights
   old night like Orpheus face to face
   with Hades creating
   his bride. Embrace.
   Basho's old frog perpetuates
   the pond. Echoes of grace.
   The moon is great with a dolphin.

3. A living ocean warms
   the growing that knows its way: a mystery
   like Mozart's geography. Each sparked note swarms
   to its own mind: memory and intention.
   Cells act out timeless fact creating forms
   of time: hands, fingers, feet in harmony.
   A person, like rhyme,
   is more than reason and the sea.

The heart has been beating for a month. The limbs
are almost ready to express the original energy.
Each sparked cell swarms to its own salt motion.

4. The eyes, unfathomable beds,
    seem underworlds where prophets and all
    the famous and sentimental dead
    recall the flood beyond Gibraltar.
    The body has no real
    skeleton. The brain shimmers in the head.
    I think of voyagers and sails
    and the bursting faces of the broad
    winds on brown old charts with whales.
    The way is round and wide
    beyond Gibraltar.

5. Remember Hartley Coleridge with maps?
    Look at this head
    and read *the eternal deep*
    which we are toiling all our lives to find.
    Here is the animate sleep
    of the planet. The blood
    vessels grip
    the brain, the skin, like the world's
    good rivers keeping
    earth and air where seeds
    and raindrops metaphrase *eternal mind.*

6. O— He is sucking
    his thumb
    and kicking
    —O!
    the limits of the garden and his luck:
    "So this is pre-existence. Give me room."
    He looks
    like an astronaut tumbling
    in the solar sack.
    He's only human.
                    O.

7. Bering Strait
    connects the northern Bering to the south end
    of the Chukchi Sea and separates,
    though frozen over from October to June,
    Capes Dezhnev and Prince of Wales. The boundary
    between Russia and US, also the International Date
    Line, pass through it. The Diomede Islands
    remain of a former landbridge. Discovered in 1648
    by Semen Dezhnev, the Bering sounds
    a maximum 170 feet
    and is frozen over from October to June.

8. He comes. Earth, air, and water.
    We have prepared the way.
    The sun rises over the parking lot.
    He comes forth like a thaw or dew
    in April. From the waiting
    room window I watch day
    break around the black crater
    of a probing chimney.
    The hospital is reflected
    in oil slicking last night's rain.
    He comes forth like a flower to be cut down.

9. I think of the chorus at Colonus speaking
    for Sophocles warning
    us back.
    I hear the laugh of Troilus at our woe.
    Worlds within worlds of perfect echo
    and embrace, dawning in dawning,
    swarm to mind: spores and planets beckon.
    Waves and horses' manes and ferns.
    Man was made to praise and reckon.
    We have flawed the waters of morning.
    I hear the laugh of Troilus at our woe.

Bric a brac

They have been two years married
and rent the house.

At one end of the sagging studio couch, a glass table
holds a lamp, green globes, peach blossoms painted
by hand, an old shoe last, a Mexican ceramic whistle,
rude walrus with the face and beard of an old man,
Mexican candlesticks, birds and birdhouses in a tree,
and dust and wax, straw flowers in carnival glass,
an Italian marble dish of *objets trouve*, old bolts,
flat nails, a cog, a starting coil, a whiffletree,
picked up along the highway or in fields, a bronzed
plaster bust from a local auction, a pre-Raphaelite
girl who sucks her lips and wears wide poppies
in her hair.

They are an unlikely couple.
Their first child, a boy,
is just learning to walk
and she is eight months pregnant.
He is an assistant professor
and can't resist the trifles of the eye.

Crickets

They invade us come Fall to die.
They swarm beneath doors, leaping
like Black Russians into corners
of the parlor, kitchen, bathroom, study,
sewing room. They do not bother or revolt
us though we have been warned
they eat the curtains, rugs, upholstery.
Spiders keep us busy anyway.
Swatters and poisoners, we
ignore the crickets.

Nights they serenade,
throwing their voices. Ventriloquists,
they are never where we and the cat
expect them. Mornings their aubades
cheer my tub. By the third week
of September their corpses strew the floor.
We get the vacuum out.

Today, while reading Horace by the potted
plants and ashtrays in the hall, I watched
a cricket reconnoiter.
Just for the hell
of it, I stamped my foot. Then
he kept close to the wall, advancing
over the bodies of his dead. At last
he made the kitchen and I turned to my book.

House Guests

We sprawl on woven longues the morning after
and the lawn sprawls weave and wave
around us. Beyond our glasses, shades
and tumblers, trees in their shadows
stand like fishers hip-booted in pools
and our boys
tumble and toss the green. I drink the day, a brew
of dandelions in a snifter, and a hair
of last night. Like my *Book of Common
Prayer*, opened beside a beetle,
things seem to be finding their place, tending
toward grass and flower, then
unfolding while our guests
nod around you,
Woman,
and our offspring
breeze the green world and yellow
wind and word. I watch
them leap and spin and fall. I leap.
I spin and fall behind my glasses
while a sunflower bows beside the wall.

Logos

Here to my hidingplace my son
brings me a turnip.

You have to see it to believe or know it.
A child does not hold—he comprehends a turnip.

I have put suicide behind me and I am not proud.
I am weary of murder in the name of law and order,

and murder in the name of revolution,
and murder in the name of god and inspiration,

and murder in the name of liberty,
and murder in the name of father, daughter, son.

We murder in the name of love.
How can the boy learn cleanness?

How can I teach him?
We have no clean names left.

He knows the touch and weight of turnips.
What harm can come of turnips?

Two for Julian and Ben

1. First Hail

We sit and watch
the glittering aggies bounce.
We listen to them pobble roof
and ping the cellar hatch.
Then Julian announces:
"God is everything."

"Did you know that?" he asks
and waits while a white
stone melts in my hand.

2. A Resurrection of the Body

Benjamin stands
beside the rainbow tub
and tells his brother:
"Look! I've got arms
and legs." Seahorse
and starfish drift
along the walls.

Taxonomy

We've tried to look
it up: that black
and yellow spider
who zips its web.

We've seen it loom
on raspberry bushes.
It favors raspberry
bushes, we assume.

Our wildlife
encyclopedia doesn't
list *raspberry*
or *zipper*, it isn't

tunnel or *trapdoor*,
we do not find it
under *garden*.
Furthermore,

John Crompton's
Life of the Spider
is missing from
my shelves or my sons'.

So, dumb we stand
again and hand
in hand with awe,
unanswered, in the wood.

A Young Raccoon

The creature was in trouble,
dying, perhaps rabid,
and we ought
to have been worried about
our boys and the neighborhood kids
who would inevitably gather
and might get bitten, but—
discovering the creature
outside our picture window,
we could not be serious.

He occupied our porch.
A yearling raccoon,
his eyes behind the bandit mask
looked drunk. He'd sit up,
ill-fitting fur like a wino's
hand-me-down topcoat,
and topple softly to the left,
sit up and topple to the right,
stagger. He was so
damned cute.

The kids did gather.
Giggles gave way to gaping.
We had to call a neighbor
to come with his shotgun.
The creature was so tractable,
so willing to roll
with a nudge from the barrel
off the stone into the grass.
Mr. Briere was efficient.
I marveled: how inappropriate we are.

Three years later, when I had
my first attacks of vertigo,
I remembered the raccoon

and how the state
game warden who came
to collect the body told us:
it sometimes happens in Spring,
they don't quite make it out
of hibernation.

.

An Afternoon with Edward Sabotka

He has barely escaped, thanks to a crashing intervention
    of the atmosphere, from being
sexually attacked by "an older woman" (she must have been
    something: a mastodon would,
I think, have hesitated to accost the Pollack) at Hubbarton
    Battlefield (idyll of the DAR)—and comes to us,
greased tail between his legs, bringing
a hard-won BO and wine breath, sorrowing
up the ass of the animal farce of all existence. In his back-
    ground—Linda (seething
where the hell he is), a junk-lumber shack, a PhD in Math
    in a jobless year. I have
Virginia with me in our contractor's brick. I seem to know
    my way around a big bad wolf. I'm fresh
from the shower and Gillette. My scamp/camp Celtic craft
    —on my father's side—rides the surface,
    sensitive and silly. Eight years
ago I taught him Milton in an evening class: *we're younger*
    than that now. In those days
Ed and Linda kept a goat. Virginia and I made babies. Now
    they keep chickens. We are performing
    in local galleries and coffee houses. Ed's
    having trouble with alcohol. I'm
    flying dry. (This stanza
counterpoints the accidents of time that have opposed
    our persons and our circumstances
    for appearances. What does it matter?
    We find our shadows in each other.
    We have both a Polish mother.)

"There comes some broad at you," he says, "and tells you
    you're attractive, she
    's attracted, and you see yourself
sitting to pinch the pimples, standing to piss in the wind."
    (And the winding sheet.) "We'd do better
to stick to ART." (And cultivate.) He mentions Mozart

(MOTS ART, Mama). I remember
he thought Milton more than Shakespeare because the epicist
        hangs on a more accessible, coherent scaffold:
        intellect. New England Puritan,
you are less ready than you seem beneath those Middle
        European muscles.

I remind him of the plots of Wolfgang's operas. "Yet art
        must be vulgar too." Ariel to Caliban. Look
        how we compensate. Virginia
        pours the coffee. Ed recalls
an afternoon with Linda in Manhattan's Central Park. A man
        in leather knickers danced a big knife
        among the crowd. The crowd
        mingled and moved on. The baboon
        in the zoo'd
been given summer squashes. He would lick his fingers then—
        "Look there! He's sketching the people."
        —doodle it on the ground floor of his cage.
        We look again: the squash
is baboon turds. The creature dabbles in the liquid
        of his proper diarrhea. He eats his own
        excrement: "*Even shit sings*. You
        said it, Edward." Then
they fell among a chanting mob at a drum concert looking
        up.

He thought it might be a rain dance. He looked up. Infinite
        flowers—
daffodils and daisies, for instance—were falling
out of the sky.
First: he felt
        he was witness to a miracle. Then: he saw
        it was another crazy put on of decaying urban culture.
        He looked for the airplane. "Oh God,"
I squeal. "If I had seen it—if I'd seen it, I'd have lost
        my mind—at last! I would have come."

Later we reminisce over Bowery panhandlers. Yes: I gave,
     I gave. What a couple
of elegant bastards! (From reading this poem
you learn that on the afternoon of July 27, 1973,
     in Castleton, VT,
     there was a storm, brief
     but electric: let it be
     remembered.)

Crystal Beach

Grass grows to the edge
against the wind. The wind
blows off the water,
reaches me between
two willows leaning
where the bank
piles highest: rocks.
Great trees and old
I think—easily
three feet thick.

Neighbors and other
strangers lie in the sun
or chat while children run
or build sand condominiums.
I listen for the wind's
own song beneath its burden
of lap and leaf and radio.

Twenty feet out
a raft rocks crowded
with young bodies.
A ball of young limbs
somersaults air.
My sons are out there hard
to spot among their peers
and the dazzle, razzmatazz
of sun and spray.
A young woman
slices into the water.

In my shade I watch.
The lake between my legs
and willows keeps
its secrets.

Weeding

The snake
stands slick and so still
I lose my faith that minutes will
pass—except the fly
reminds me as he
flirts at the serpent
head, lights on the dragon
eye, flickers and ticks
about its slag
slate patio (like small
Saint George or children while
their parents stoop to grace
before a meal) playing
the fool, playing
for time, a very ancient

game. And I kneel
at a little distance
forgetting to pull
the next weed.

Perspectives

Last summer butterflies
surfaced unutterable: Monarch,
Vanessa, Swallowtail. God
plunged both arms down my throat,
tugging out heart and stomach.
"Pah!—a painted bug."
I matched my common sense
to bliss and saved my life.

This winter I stagger down snow
on mountain pass and ponder
the sleep of bears.

Glass

A litter of evening
grosbeaks, black and yellow,
strews the grass
and pavement beside our new
humanities hall that, mostly glass,
stands directly in the path
of their migration south.

There's one turns up
a breast for my inspection
from the faculty lounge.
Professors Stagg and Onion,
discovering the object of my gaze,
say: *sad*—and I sigh:
yes—and then we draw
a cup of coffee, slip
into the lavatory, stride
into supplies.

I cannot turn
my fancy with my eyes
away. I can imagine
flight, the promise of a winter
paradise, the whole idea of sky,
the small bird
brain, but air!
turned suddenly to barrier
is an enormity, stunning
and impossible as memory
or simply death.

I catch myself recalling
old woodcuts or, on icons,
the paraclete: a pigeon
sliding down the golden stair
toward pentecost, everything

rather stilted and divine
and right as the roar
of john or whirr of ditto
accosting me like feathers
through an open door.

Panto

Our weatherperson promised rain. I'm out
walking anyway. Sodden, I watch
a stranger mongrel study my approach
beneath the windblown porous bumbershoot.
Our distance narrows. He decides. I shout.
The jaws and muddy paws encroach, but lurch
right by. Behind, I feel cold nose and snatch
my hand away. "No, stop!" Obnoxious lout—

I don't look back, assume he's gone. Later,
he passes me again. He won't look back.
Now I observe he's missing a right hind leg.
My god! How well he trots! as if the lack
were nothing. Now he stops beside a gate
and lifts the invisible member like a brag.

Leaving the Campus

After a late meeting
of the faculty committee on student life,
I swing the old buick through the gateposts
onto Seminary Street.

My headlights sweep
old clapboard, tunnel between old trees,
and barely catch the apparent freshman
sleep-

walking as it seems
toward the conscious edge of my right eye,
a pretty face, a body like the grace early
Aegean dreamers

raised from stone,
the six pack budding at his fingertips,
stilled arc of his right arm.
He looks lonely,

a hunter, scared
and surly, young,
so full of emptiness
he dares

the world to do—
something? Anything. I try to remember that
I wasted once in deserts without salt
and crossed somehow.

Is it that rapture
and pain finally shame us out? I want
to tell him but— he's passed the gates
and doesn't need my crap.

Remembering Julia
(1997)

"They are all gone into the world of light"
    —Henry Vaughan

She is now gone. Maybe the speed of light
detains her. I don't know—as "I don't know"
was her refrain expressing, we guessed, the bite
of digestive juices loosed and raging through
her body, her delirium, her last
week in the world. Then, from her stupor, she
awoke, girlish almost, almost the ghost
she had been seeking, finding instead: "My three
best bums..." she said. Her grandsons and their dad
(I am their dad)—we hovered round her head
like angels. All the generations had
gathered, women and men, beside her bed,
even three little boys. She drew me in,
questing, to question: "How do I begin?"

ENVOYS

Stanzas on My Name
(1956)

Within the alchemy of nouns a name
is something rude and real and works, its fame
and influence like stars; the journeyman
apprenticed to our flesh who works in flame
to crease our hands, to forge the gold of plan
upon our days according to each line,
our form out of our fire. Surely my
first burning was ambiguous and came
of vague and many, commonplace: so I
was named, as Thomas is, a twin, not one.
Then Smith is work and fun for everyman.

The blacksmith, brazened of the sun, from steel
shapes blazing shoes; when horses come and kneel,
dark in his hand, he seems one sheen with them,
and stern, upon one furnace formed. The sil-
versmith, with hair like moonlight, is the gem
that burns in his design, that is of him
his burning true and pallid in an urn
like pale old men. The goldsmith cannot feel
another heat than his own dazzle borne
on gorgeous scabbard and a golden blade;
in this swift fire he has lived and died.

A smith is one who works a thing from fire,
who rescues and informs some shape of fair
or useful with his fury or the moons
and silver of his pallor. Words require
something from our center, some of man's
excess and mystery—the deep expense
of use and elegance. Our form is found,
a fire out of fire, laying bare
the black and silver, gold and diamond.
And diamond's the stone that burns of earth,
its womb of fire, ore, its flaming smith.

A name inspires holocausts and myth,
and every noun's a name: my name is Smith
because the soul is fire and the womb's
a burning and my flesh is burning with
its form, and every flesh the soul informs
with burning hardens burning and assumes
its shape, and names its burning with a noun.
My name is Smith for burning from my birth
to work with fire. Smith is everyman
and I, who burn all names and nouns to praise,
the ode our burning hardens to a blaze.

The ode is static, faceted, is made
and moves like diamond, a flame as hard,
as single and as imperceptible:
its silences, continuous and proud,
as furious: its shaft, equivocal.
My burning, apprehensive, very still,
has black and silver, gold and diamonds
in it, that is hardened to the deed
and good of heroes. Making saints, of wounds
and blisses, is the blessing in a name
that works, like stars, its influence and fame.

The noun a name is burns to make its myth.
Odes burden me whose name is triply Smith.
Maddened at common ores, the alchemist
Sings angels from the flesh that I have kissed.
My birth's most fabled beast is burning with
Its legend in my breast. I'm wrought, at last,
To love my name, the all, and every smith
Having aspired. Man, I am, and myth.

A Poet at Seventy Years
(March 2003)

And his parents have closed their books.
(Not that they ever read much. Does anyone?)
He thinks of them moldering between covers.
At least he saw to their planting side by side
as perhaps they would have wished. It is good,
he supposes, to have achieved the ideal
indifference of the dead.

At thirty-five, that watershed, he adopted an attitude
of dutiful scion, married and himself a parent, embarked
upon straight years and narrow. He sits hunched (here's
another thirty-five) over his pages, eyes closed, fingers
cold against his cheekbones, thumbs
supporting a failing jawline, dewlaps
warming inside his palms. He wonders,
like any ordinary person, or some poet,
what has happened to the years, what
does he want to confess or withhold.

At seventeen, he deified Rimbaud,
enfant terrible of French poetry, all poetry: poetry is
a foreign language, infant's babble, sibilance
of androgyns, verbal revenge for the abuses suffered
at seven from the mouths and hands and genitals
of bullies and public school-teachers and purveyors
of penny candy. He took to heart the worlds
of MGM and Warner Bros. while sadsack dusty
moths materialized out of the darkness beside him
in the fleabag moviehouse. On Sunday mornings
he ate God and inhaled the pomp of incense
and candles, priest and altar boys and nuns. At length,
he cultivated a flirt's passivity
assaulting the conventional sensibilities of parents
and peers and principals. Later,
he squandered himself, wayward and unruly, self-

destructive, addicted to alcohol and razor blades,
neo-classic, ultra-conservative, self-loathing, formalist, caring
profoundly for assonance, metaphor, irony, rhyme.
At last, he had to save his life. The muse insisted.

In his dotage now, of course, he dotes
on sons and grandsons, handsome and bright,
at home in the world at hand.
("The soul selects its own society.")

The old man putters about house and garden.
He has recently taken up the ballet. Three times weekly,
at the barre, across the floor, he fancies himself a fat
old seal cavorting on the rocks.
He is deaf in one ear. He expects
soon to be blind altogether.
He has become a funny fellow re-enacting
the Irish grampa of his childhood, the jigging wildman
resurrected in a latter-day sobriety. Every morning,

the old man descends to his workspace in the cellar
to make poetry: poems celebrating rock
stars, serial killers, tabloid sensations, every
day things like the neckties in his closet,
spider on the windshield,
rubber chicken, colonoscopy.

Senex terrible! Anchored in his quiet harbor
at the end of the world, he has freed himself
of loathings and addictions. He has let go
of everything but family and poetry.
He could let go of poetry
and float away
finding some lesser freedom like the sky.